Richard Scarry's

Best First Book
Ever

First published in hardback by HarperCollins *Publishers* in 1980
This edition published by HarperCollins *Children's Books* in 2013

HarperCollins *Children's Books* is a division of HarperCollins *Publishers* Ltd,
77-85 Fulham Palace Road, London W6 8JB

1 3 5 7 9 10 8 6 4 2

ISBN: 978-0-00-749165-0

The HarperCollins website address is www.harpercollins.co.uk

Printed and bound in China.

Richard Scarry's
Best First Book
Ever

HarperCollins *Children's Books*

Busytown

library

road mender

street cleaner

CAFÉ

BOOKS

Postman Pig

shopkeeper

This is a street in Busytown.
My! What a busy town.
Mummy, Daddy, Huckle, and
Sally Cat live in Busytown. Their
friend Lowly Worm does, too.
Something is always happening here.

bumper

traffic lights

Mr. frumble

CLOTHING

BARBER

scissors

shopper

baby

pushchair

barber

Oh dear! The wind blew Mr. Frumble's hat away. *Catch it, Mr. Frumble!*

SUPERMARKET

steeple

church

pavement

greengrocer

butcher

customer

windscreen

headlight

motorcycle

Sergeant Murphy

tyre

pickle car

milk float

MAIN STREET   OKAY SQUARE

street sign

POST OFFICE

FIRE STATION

pole

sign

TAXI

TAXI STAND

post van

fire engine

fireman

The Cat Family

This is the house of the Cat family –
Daddy, Mummy, Huckle and Sally.
Their friend Lowly Worm often comes
to spend the night.

roof

Huckle Cat's
bedroom

Sally Cat

bathroom

Huckle

blanket

Lowly Worm

side
of the
house

bed

landing

clock

back door

sink

cabinets

bush

kitchen floor

table

stairs

chimney

attic window

The sun is coming up.
It is almost daylight.
Wake up, Cat family!

weather vane

dy cat

lamp

Mummy Cat

rising
sun

table

wardrobe

picture

candle

garage

hat

fireplace

vase

car

television

logs

sofa

rug

books

front door

living room

bookcase

front lawn

Mr. Fr

In the Bathroom

The Cat family wakes up.
They take turns using
the bathroom.

mirror

medicine cabinet

glass

soap

Daddy Cat washes
his face.

dressing gown

wash basin

shower

shower
curtain

tap

bathtub

Mummy Cat takes
a shower.

pyjamas

comb

bath mat

perfume

talcum powder

toothpaste

shampoo

Huckle brushes
his teeth.

nightgown

slippers

Sally combs her hair.

scales

toilet

And Lowly Worm weighs himself.
How much do you weigh, Lowly?

Getting Dressed

Now they all get dressed.

Daddy puts on his best blue suit and his favourite red tie.

Sally's hat

Daddy's hat   Huckle's cap

jacket

shirt

trousers   shoes

Huckle wears a yellow shirt. He pulls on his red dungarees.

underpants

socks

plimsolls

My! Doesn't Sally look nice in her green pinafore dress and black shoes?

Lowly ties his one shoelace.

Mummy Cat is having a hard time deciding what to wear.
She finally decides to wear a skirt and a blouse.

scarf

handkerchief

slip

trousers   skirt   blouse   sweater

dress

handbag

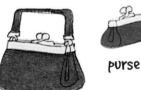
purse

tights

shoes   boots   sandals

salad bowl

refrigerator

wall cabinet

jar

tin

packet

eggs

milk

ice cubes

meat

leftovers

door

cheese

bottles

lettuce

freezer

MARCH

1 2 3
4 5 6 7 8 9 10
11 12 13 14 15 16 17
18 19 20 21 22 23 24
25 26 27 28 29 30 31

calendar

clock

milk
bread
butter

shopping
list

pencil

coffeepot

teapot

fork

plate

knife

spoon

sugar bowl

salt

pepp

napkin

tablecloth

mop

chair

jug

cereal bowl

grater

egg beater

bottle opener

wire whisk

Breakfast in the Kitchen

Mummy is frying bacon and eggs.
Sally is making toast.
Huckle is pouring milk into his cereal bowl.
Oh dear! Lowly fell in! Hurry,
Huckle! Wash him off in the sink.

Mr. Frumble

cooker hood

curtains

iron

bread

rolls

scales

table

egg cup

bottle

ironing board

saucepan

chopping board

mug

laundry basket

frying pan

kettle

burnt toast

hot plate

glass

cup

sponge

washing-up liquid

saucer

apron

tap

toaster

eggshells

sink

butter

mincer

brush

ladle

strainer

rolling pin

spatula

measuring spoons

colander

carving knife

paring knife

Housework

After breakfast everyone helps with the housework. Lowly helps clear the table. Be careful, Lowly. Daddy washes the dishes.

keys

lamp

lemo\
squeez

rubbish bin

pots and pans

Sally sweeps the floor.

Huckle holds the dustpan.

bucke\
wat

broom

dustpan

scrubbing brush

washing liquid

Mummy washes the laundry.\
The washing machine is leaking, Mummy.\
Daddy slips on the wet floor.

shelf

watch

mop

washing machine

laundry basket

Sally will mop up the water.

After Lowly made all the beds, his own bed looked so nice that he decided to take a nap.
Daddy is vacuuming the living-room carpet. My! That vacuum cleaner certainly is hungry!
Sally dusts the room.

staircase

umbrella stand

chest of drawers

armchair

feather duster

television

record player

telephone

bookcase

camera

magazines

Huckle empties the wastepaper basket.

books

Mummy is sewing a shirt for Lowly.

radio

pins

safety pin

spool of thread

buttons

pin cushion

thimble

sewing machine

scissors

table

tape measure

rose

vase

Miss Honey

drawing pins

pushpin

bell

map

notice

lost
plimsoll

notice board

pad of
paper

ruler

1 2 3 4 5

pencil
sharpener

pen

table

piano

singer

At School

Huckle, Sally and Lowly
go to school. They do many
things at school.
This morning, Miss Honey,
the teacher, is playing
a tune on the piano and
singing a song.

embroidery

colouring book

crayons

glue

scrapbook

sheet of paper

stool

paint box

scraps of paper

water dish

footprint

maths lesson

spelling lesson

blackboard

blackboard duster

chalk

Mr. Frumble

writing on the blackboard

reading a picture book

stringing beads

sink

Caretaker Joe keeps the school neat and clean. Ooops! He slipped on a bead.

mop

bucket of water

wastepaper basket

pencil

rubber

marker pen

picture

a picture painter

sticky tape

paint jars

Sizes

Miss Honey is teaching the children about sizes and shapes. Just look at all the sizes and shapes in the classroom.

Bug is little.

Mr. Frumble's hat is not too big and not too small. It is medium.

Miss Honey is big.

Mouse has a short nose.

Elephant has a long nose.

Some books are wide.

Some books are narrow.

Elephant has thick legs.

Spoonbill has thin legs.

Some pupils are tall.

Some pupils are short.

Hilda is big.

Bugdozer is tiny.

This cap is the right size.

This cap is too large.

Shapes

This shape is round.

Clocks are round.

The sun is round.

Buttons... coins... and wheels are round.

Lowly kicks a round ball.

A balloon is round.

Oranges are round, too.

This is a square.

A hopscotch court has lots of squares.

These blocks are square on all sides.

This is a triangle.

This flag is a triangle.

This pupil wears a paper hat that is shaped like a triangle.

This is a star.

Miss Honey gives gold stars for good schoolwork.

This is a diamond.

This is a cone.

Kites are often diamond-shaped.

Always carry your ice-cream cone this way up – if you want to eat it.

This is an oval.

An egg is oval-shaped – unless you drop it.

Then it is scrambled.

This is a heart.

Many valentines are heart-shaped.

This is a pyramid.

Lowly can make many shapes.

crooked

curved

straight

Bugdozer makes a pyramid with sand.

At the Playground

At playtime Miss Honey takes the children outside to play in the playground. No-one stays inside the school. What is everyone doing?

caretaker Joe swinging way up high

Joe's mop and bucket falling down

Sally is playing with a skipping rope.

hanging upside down

sliding down the pole

climbing up the ladder

These children are playing ring-a-ring-o'roses.

This looks like a game of leapfrog.

leaping over

behind

Two children are playing a game of tag.

in front

up

crouching down

down

This is a seesaw.

These pupils are wrestling – and getting dirty!

Two teams are playing tug-of-war.

losers

winners

top of slide

bottom of slide

Miss Honey takes a turn sliding down the slide.

Lowly is playing hide-and-seek.

inside the barrel

outside the barrel

kick

on the left

in the middle

on the right

Three children are standing side by side.

ball

catch

throw

miss

hit

hat

somersaulting

going in

coming out

Two pupils are in the sandpit.

play house

Is Mr. Frumble still chasing his hat?
Catch it, Mr. Frumble!

The Alphabet

A a — aeroplane

B b — boat

C c — crab

D d — dog

E e — engine

F f — frumble

G g — goose

H h — hen

I i — igloo

J j — jeep

K k — kangaroo

L l — letter

M m — motorcycle

After playtime Lowly reads his ABC book.
Do you know your ABCs?

N n nurse

O o owl

P p penguin

Q q queen

R r rooster

S s sparrow

T t turtle

U u umbrella

V v van

W w wolf

X x xylophone

Y y yak

Z z zebra

Counting

Mummy and Daddy pick up the children after school. They have many errands to do before going home. The children practise counting along the way.

1 one window cleaner

2 two police officers

3 three street cleaners

4 four schoolchildren waiting for their buses

BUS 1 BUS 2 BUS 3 BUS 4

5 five bicycle riders

six painters

seven postmen and women

eight pencil cars

nine bug taxis

ten firefighters putting out a fire

My! What a lot of firefighters!

Colours

On the way to town, Huckle and Lowly see cars and trucks of many different colours. Their own car is orange.

a red fire engine

a yellow bananamobile

an orange school bus

a green watermelon truck

Red and yellow make orange.

Blue and yellow make green.

Red and blue make purple.

Red and white make pink.

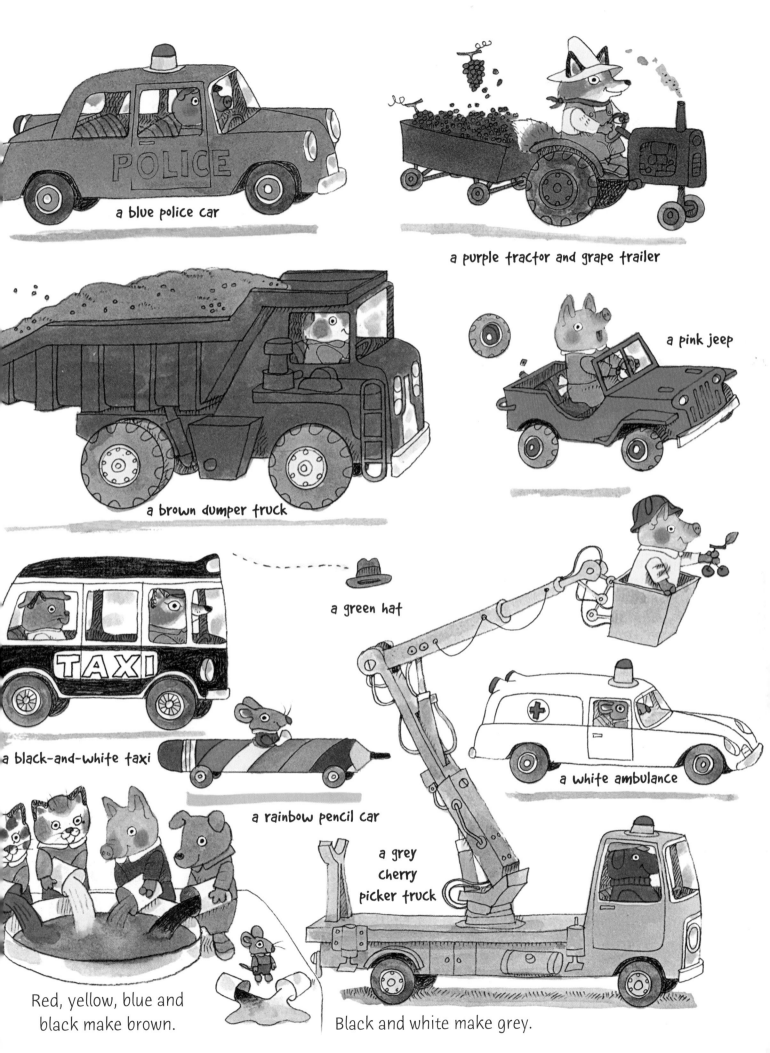

a blue police car

a purple tractor and grape trailer

a brown dumper truck

a pink jeep

a green hat

a black-and-white taxi

a rainbow pencil car

a white ambulance

a grey cherry picker truck

Red, yellow, blue and black make brown.

Black and white make grey.

FRUITS

bananas

Grocer Dog

lemons · apples · oranges · cherries · grapefruit · grapes

pears · melons · strawberries · blueberries · raspberries · pineapple

pickle barrel

watermelon

At the Supermarket

The Cat family stops at the supermarket. Daddy buys fresh fruit and vegetables from the greengrocer. Mummy buys some meat from the butcher.

hook

saw

ham

meat cleaver

mincing machine

bacon

sausages

minced meat

string

chop

steak

smoked sausage

knife

apron

knife sharpener

roll of pap

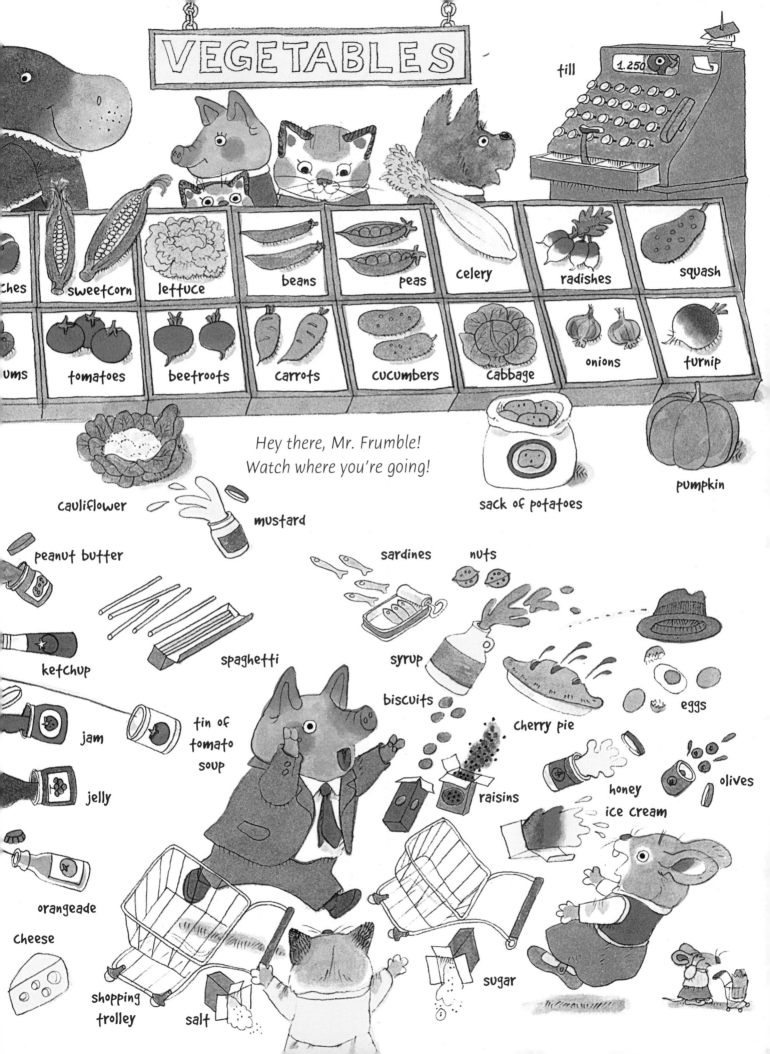

VEGETABLES

till

...ches sweetcorn lettuce beans peas celery radishes squash

...ums tomatoes beetroots carrots cucumbers cabbage onions turnip

Hey there, Mr. Frumble!
Watch where you're going!

sack of potatoes

pumpkin

cauliflower

mustard

peanut butter

sardines   nuts

spaghetti

syrup

biscuits

cherry pie

eggs

ketchup

jam

tin of
tomato
soup

raisins

honey   olives

jelly

ice cream

orangeade

cheese

shopping
trolley   salt

sugar

Good and Bad Manners

After putting their shopping into the car, the Cat family decides to go to the ice-cream parlour for a treat. There they meet Mrs. Pig and her two boys.

"How do you do, Mrs. Pig?" says Huckle. "I would do much better if Bop and Biff would stop fighting and mind their manners," says Mrs. Pig.

Lowly sits up straight in his chair like a good worm.

Sally says politely, "Please pass the biscuits."

When Huckle is served, he says, "Thank you."

Bop and Biff fight over who is going to have which chair. *Naughty boys!*

Lowly eats slowly and quietly.

Bop gobbles his ice cream and makes awful noises.

Biff doesn't ask someone to pass the biscuits. He reaches over to get them and knocks over Bop's juice.

Biff guzzles his juice and spills it all over his shirt. You should take smaller sips, Biff!

Mrs. Pig is talking to Mummy Cat. Bop keeps interrupting his mother, which is not very nice manners.

Huckle has more cherries than Sally. He shares his cherries with her.

Biff steals the cherries from Bop's ice cream. What an awful thing to do!

Don't rock back and forth in your chair, Biff! It is not good manners.

He rocks too far and grabs the tablecloth.

Biff clears the table. What terrible manners!

And what a mess! You will have to teach your boys better manners, Mrs. Pig.

As he leaves, Lowly says, "It was nice to meet you, Mrs. Pig. And good luck with your manners lessons."

A Visit to the Doctor

Today Huckle has an appointment for a check-up with Dr. Bones.

After Huckle takes off his clothes, Dr. Bones listens to Huckle's heart through his stethoscope. "Your heart is thumping very nicely, Huckle," says Dr. Bones.

Lowly steps on the scales. "You have put on some weight since the last time you were here, Lowly," says Nurse Nora.

Dr. Bones measures Huckle's height. "My, you are growing tall," he says. "You must be eating everything your mother serves you."

Next Dr. Bones checks Huckle's eyesight. "I can see everything on the chart," says Huckle. "You have very good eyes," says Dr. Bones.

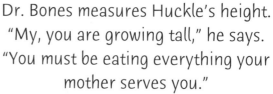

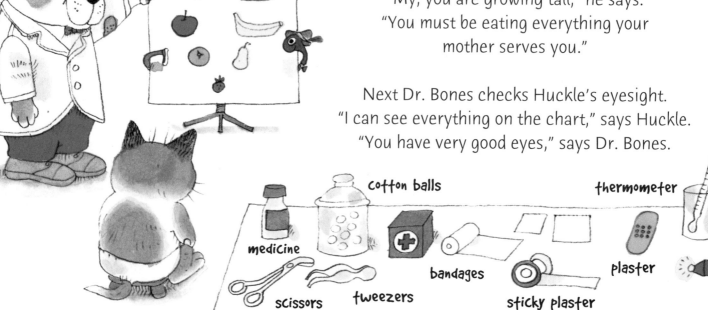

cotton balls

thermometer

medicine

bandages

plaster

scissors   tweezers   sticky plaster   torch

spatula

"I must give you a vaccination to keep you healthy," says Dr. Bones. "It may hurt a little bit, but only for a second." It doesn't hurt too much.

Then Dr. Bones looks at Huckle's throat. He also looks at Lowly's throat. "Say AH-H-H, Lowly." Lowly says, "AH-H-H." "You have a very nice long throat, Lowly."

Dr. Bones taps on Huckle's back. He looks in Huckle's ears. He squeezes Huckle's tummy a little bit. "That tickles," says Huckle.

"Well, Huckle," says Dr. Bones, "it has been a pleasure to examine such a fine, healthy boy as you. You may get dressed now."

As Huckle and Lowly leave, Dr. Bones says, "Keep eating properly and I am sure that you will be much bigger on your next visit." "Goodbye, and thank you, Dr. Bones."

The Parts of the Body

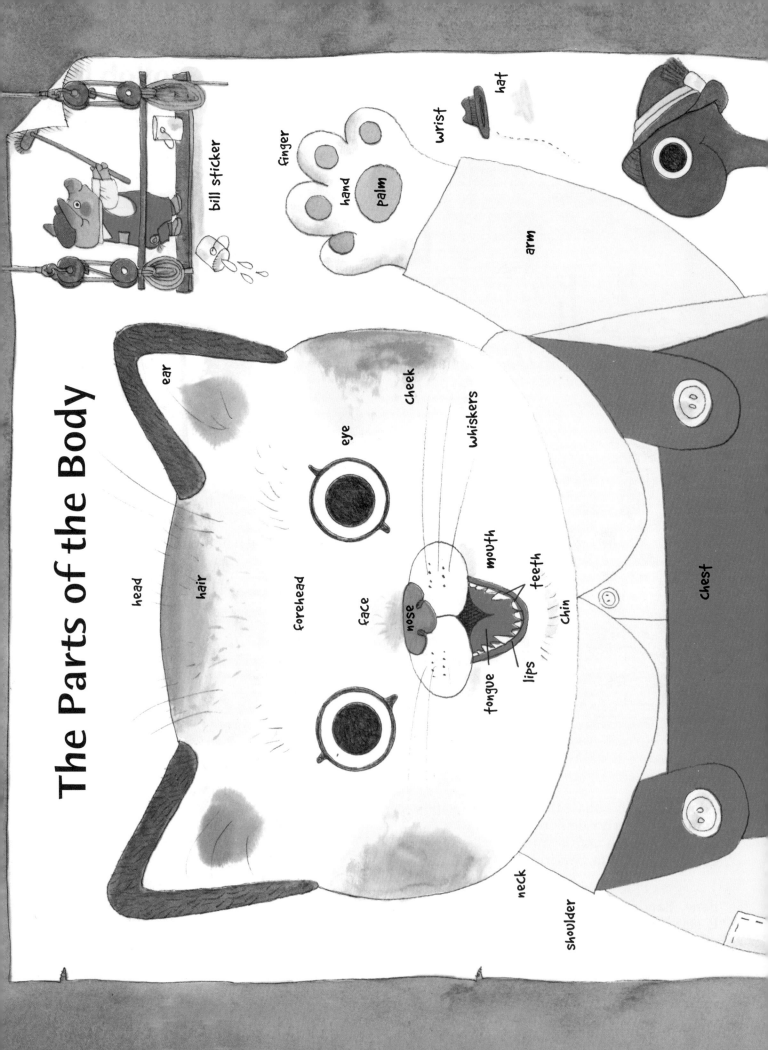

jacket

back

trousers

shoe

shoelace

tail

hip

wall

leg

foot

toe

stomach

waist

heel

As the Cat family drives
along they see a poster
of Huckle and Lowly. It
shows the parts of the body.
"Wow! I'm big!" says Lowly.

ankle

knee

hand

Farmer Pig's Farm

helicopter

sky

mountains

cloud

aeroplane

woods

hill

lake

meadow

wheat field

gate

stone wall

scarecrow

sweetcorn store

sweetcorn field

weather vane

N E S W

plough

tractor

silo

hayloft

vegetable garden

rooster

fence

barn

rope

load

sickle

hoe   scythe   rake   pitchfork   ladder   sack   barrel

hen

baby chick

Mr. frumble

rowing boat

bridge

forest

windmill

apple tree

brook

grain harvester

chimney

"Let's visit Farmer Pig
and his family and see
what they are doing,"
says Daddy.
My! What a busy farm.
They are growing all kinds
of things to eat.

farmhouse

water pump

apple pie

axe

"But where are all your
children, Mrs. Pig? And what
are they doing?" asks Daddy.

well

woodpile

grass cutter

"They are all in the next
field," says Mrs. Pig.
"Come, I will show you
what they are doing."

a pick-up truck that
reversed too far

stream

Action Words

Farmer and Mrs. Pig certainly have a lot of children. And they are all doing something.

eating

drinking

standing

sitting

lying down

holding and smelling

pushing

riding

pulling

talking

listening

kneeling

laughing

smiling

frowning

crying

walking

running

jumping

shouting

whispering

giggling

tripping

hiding

reading

writing

drawing

watching

falling

giving

taking

digging

building

pointing

looking

sewing

blowing

singing and dancing

kicking

kissing

hugging

wrestling

Lowly is wriggling.

And what is Mr. Frumble doing?
Why, Mr. Frumble is still
chasing his hat!
I wonder if he will ever catch it.

At the Harbour

barge

funnel

towline

tugboat

rowing boat

submarine

lighthouse

rocks

pier

sailing boat

"We mustn't forget to stop at the fish market," says Mummy. "I haven't forgotten," says Daddy. "Here we are at the harbour now."

buoy

speeding motorboat

fishing boat

water taxi

Mr. frumble

Mummy buys fresh fish for supper. "That is the last of our shopping," she says. "Now we can go straight home."

a fisherman mending his net

net

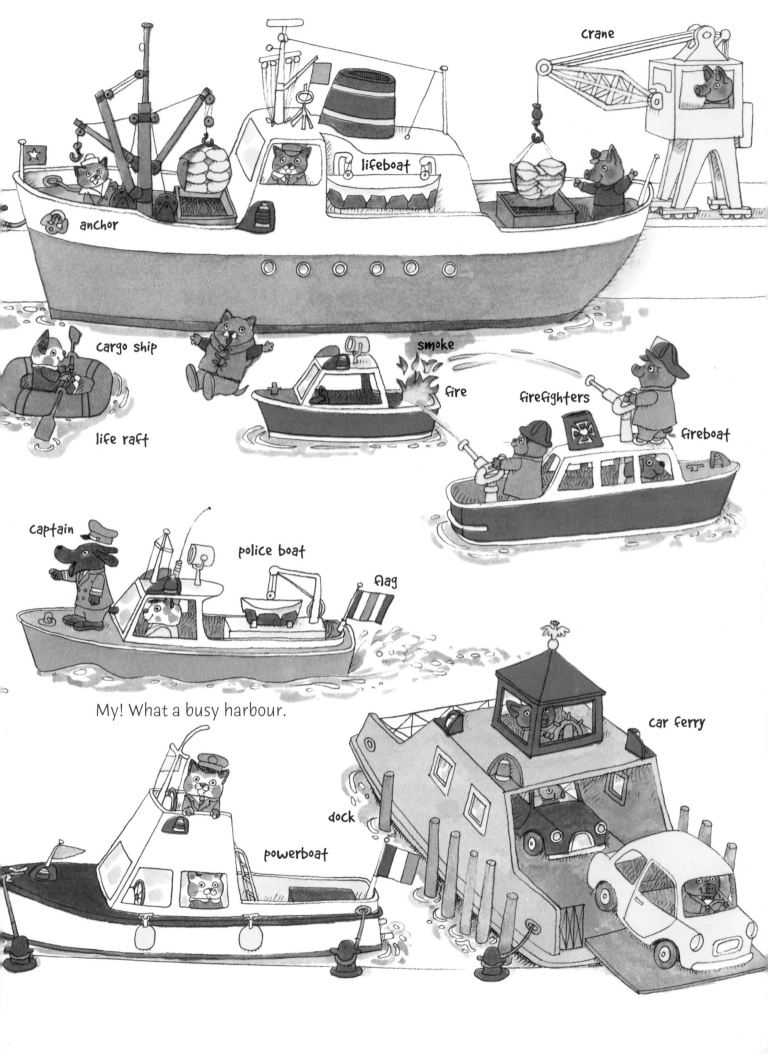

crane

lifeboat

anchor

cargo ship

smoke

fire

firefighters

fireboat

life raft

captain

police boat

flag

My! What a busy harbour.

car ferry

dock

powerboat

The Railway Station

On the way home, the Cat family has to pass the railway station. As they approach the crossing, the guards crank down the crossing gates. STOP! Two trains are coming into the station!

signal box

level crossing gate

BAGG

road

station platform

railway tracks

fried eggs

waiter

COACH

RESTAURANT C

APPLE JUICE

snack stall

warning sign

repair worker

railway station

signal light

BUSYTOWN

closed van

TICKETS

1

1

mail bags

steam
locomotive

diesel locomotive

buffer

fork-lift truck

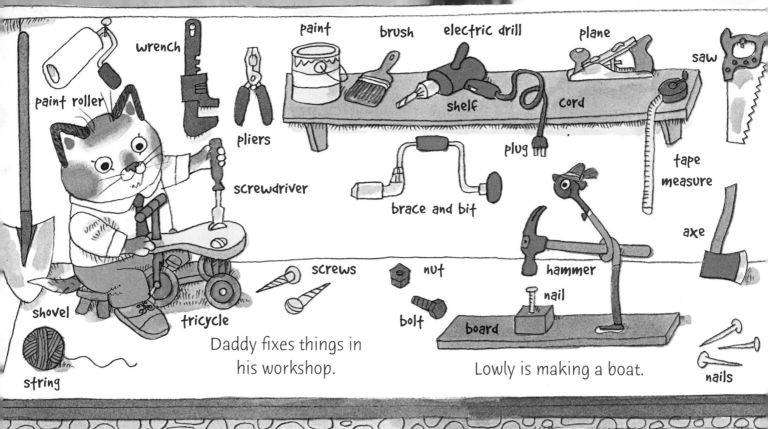

paint roller
wrench
paint
brush
electric drill
plane
saw
pliers
shelf
cord
screwdriver
plug
tape measure
brace and bit
axe
shovel
screws
nut
hammer
nail
tricycle
bolt
board
nails
string

Daddy fixes things in his workshop.

Lowly is making a boat.

In the Garden

The Cat family arrives home at last.
But there are still many chores to do around the house.
Daddy has asked some workers to come over and help.

watering can

clover

flowerpot

hoe

trowel

tap

crocus

daffodil

hyacinth

strawberry

tulip

pansies

hose

bluebells

violets

lilies of the valley

daisies

roses

bug

Mummy waters the flowers in her garden.
Watch what you're doing, Mummy.

sunflower

leaf

leaves

branch

trunk

tree

Sally picks
a basket
of flowers.

sack

rock

Freddy Fox is on
the stepladder picking
apples from the
apple tree.
I hope he doesn't
hurt himself.

stepladder

Oh dear! Mr. Fumble
is still trying to catch his hat!

dandelion

The boy from next door is
mowing the lawn for Daddy.

Huckle rakes
the cut grass.

watch

grass

flower basket

soil

wheelbarrow

lawn mower

wagon

Mother Goose Rhymes

When supper is finished
it is night-time.
Then Daddy reads some
Mother Goose rhymes to
Sally, Huckle and Lowly.

Tom, Tom, the piper's son,
Stole a pig and away did run.
The pig was eat, and Tom was beat,
And Tom went crying down the street.

Doctor Foster went to Gloucester
In a shower of rain.
He stepped in a puddle,
Right up to his middle,
And never went there again.

Jack, be nimble.
Jack, be quick.
Jack, jump over
The candlestick.

Jack Sprat could eat no fat,
His wife could eat no lean,
And so between them both, you see,
They licked the platter clean.

Little Miss Muffet
Sat on a tuffet,
Eating her curds and whey;
Along came a spider,
Who sat down beside her,
And frightened Miss Muffet away.

Jack and Jill went up the hill
To fetch a pail of water;
Jack fell down and broke his crown,
And Jill came tumbling after.

Georgie Porgie, pudding and pie,
Kissed the girls and made them cry;
When the boys came out to play,
Georgie Porgie ran away.

Mr. Frumble

Then, after a very busy day,
everyone gets ready for bed.
Look! Mummy has fallen
asleep already!
Good night, Mummy.

Good night, sleep tight,
Wake up bright
In the morning light.

newspaper

picture book

doll

January

January is the month for coasting down snowy hills.

February

In February we give valentines to the ones we love.

March

When strong March winds blow, you should hold on to your hat.

April

Don't get wet in the April showers.

May

In May, flowers are blooming everywhere. Huckle gives a bouquet of flowers to his mother.

June

It is nice to take a drive in the country in June.

July

In hot July it is pleasant to have a picnic under a shady tree.

August

The best way to spend an August day is swimming at the beach.

September

In September Miss Honey is happy to see all her pupils return to school.

October

October is the month of falling leaves. It is fun to play in them.

November

Lowly celebrates his birthday in November. When is your birthday?

December

In December Santa Claus comes with presents for all good girls and boys.